WILL THE REAL FIRST TEN PRESIDENTS PLEASE STAND UP?

A Children's Book of Verse

Written and Illustrated by Milo Kearney

Will the Real First Ten Presidents Please Stand Up?
Copyright ©2018, Milo Kearney
Illustrations © 2018, Milo Kearney
Pukiyari Publishers

ISBN-10: 1-63065-108-7
ISBN-13: 978-1-63065-108-4

PUKIYARI PUBLISHERS
www.pukiyari.com

This book is dedicated to our children Kathleen and Sean
and grandchildren Ben, Eli, Ian, Jeremy, and Collin
remembering when they were small
and to a kind lady, Aunt Jean,
who devoted her life and career to second graders.
Also with great appreciation to my dear little poet Vivian
and to our daughter-in-law Lisa and son-in-law Danny.

Introduction

Who was the first President of the United States?
  It wasn't George Washington, who was a decade late.

We call the first ten Presidents simply
  Presidents of Congress even though they bore the title
  of Presidents of the United States,
  acknowledged by Washington, as should seem vital.

Our first constitution, called the Articles of Confederation,
  was drafted by John Dickinson,
  and modeled after the British nation,
  after the government of Virginia, designed by Thomas Jefferson,
  and that of Pennsylvania, designed by Benjamin Franklin.

Why don't we know our history?
Why make it such a mystery?

It is said that our first Constitution was inadequate,
  and that the first ten Presidents were less prominent,
  but does that warrant relegating the latter to oblivion
  and the former to contempt?

PRESIDENT OF THE UNITED STATES

SAMUEL HUNTINGTON

President Samuel Huntington
(March-July 1781)

So let's meet our first President,
   none other than Samuel Huntington,
   a lawyer from Connecticut,
   a self-taught and self-made man.

His birth house in Scotland, Connecticut,
   is honored as a national shrine.
   He joined the Revolution
   and became Connecticut's governor in time.

Chosen as President of the Provisional Congress,
   he became President of the U.S. in March of 1781,
   when that body became the National Congress,
   for not until November were its first elections begun.

He spent his time in office
   Seeking foreign loans to win the war.
   But in July his health broke down
   and he resigned, not up to more.

Yorktown

Thomas McKean

President Thomas McKean
(July-November 1781)

Thomas McKean took on the office,
   filling out the four months left
   until the formally chosen Congress
   could choose whom it found best.

A lawyer from the state of Delaware,
   he was the first person to try
   to point out that the Declaration of Independence was
     signed
   on January 19, 1777, not in 1776 on the fourth of July.

He was known for his honesty and efficiency.
   Yet he was criticized by John Jay
   for his close cooperation with France,
   but the Americans won at Yorktown in this way.

JOHN HANSON

ROBERT MORRIS

President John Hanson
(November 1781-November 1782)

John Hanson was a merchant from the state of Maryland,
   presiding over the first U.S. Congress so elected.
   He obtained good peace terms from the British,
   and made the new government respected.

Two factions fought each other,
   Banker Robert Morris wanted more power at the top,
   while Jefferson and Ben Franklin opposed him
   in a clash that would not stop.

Morris dominated the new Bank of North America,
   Approved to manage finances alone,
   while, as Secretary of the Treasury,
   he printed money on his own.

ELIAS BOUDINOT

THE FLIGHT FROM THE STATE HOUSE

President Elias Boudinot
(November 1782-November 1783)

From an old Huguenot family,
  His wealth influenced his political view.
  So he thought God Himself ordained the world
  to be governed by a chosen few.

In Elizabethtown, New Jersey,
  Boudinot had practiced law,
  and, as a trustee of Princeton College,
  its decisions oversaw.

His lack of sympathy with the common folk
  brought him to dismiss
  most of the Revolutionary army
  without their pay, which was amiss.

So there marched on Philadelphia.
  some 80 soldiers or more
  who then stormed into the State House,
  while Congress fled out the back door.

In no way moved by pity,
  Boudinot had George Washington
  crush the mutiny with floggings,
  and moved the capitol to Princeton.

THE NEW CINCINNATUS

THOMAS MIFFLIN

President Thomas Mifflin
(November 1783-November 1784)

A wealthy Philadelphia merchant,
    college-trained, then given a European tour,
    the Pacifist Quakers drummed Mifflin out of church
    for joining Washington's staff and fighting in the war.

Killing a proposal to hold down prices,
    Mifflin moved the capital to Annapolis in Maryland
    and then on to Trenton, New Jersey,
    away from unruly soldier bands.

Washington sent a letter to the states
    calling for a stronger type of rule,
    a plan backed by the new Cincinnati Order,
    with Alexander Hamilton its propagandist tool.

Washington was called the new Cincinnatus,
    who'd once saved ancient Rome.
    Although he later denied he would ever be king,
    rumor said this plan had been known.

But news of the scheme caused a hue and cry,
    led by Jefferson, writing home from France.
    so the Cincinnati disbanded their order
    and waited for another good chance.

RICHARD Henry Lee
DISMISSES MORRIS

President Richard Henry Lee
(November 1784-November 1785)

From the eminent Virginia planter family,
  which later produced Robert E. Lee,
  Richard Henry Lee was educated in England,
  and shared Thomas Jefferson's ideology.

Lee had helped set up the Articles of Confederation,
  and called for the expansion of slavery to be banned.
  He moved the capital to New York City,
  feeling at ease with the common man.

As President, Lee discovered that Robert Morris
  owed the government immense unaccounted funds
  and dismissed him as Secretary of the Treasury
  to stop his shenanigans.

President John Hancock
(November 1785-May 1786)

John Hancock was a mover and shaker
   leading into the Revolution,
   smuggling goods into the colonies
   despite the official British restriction.

His stand had been supported
   by the Sons of Liberty,
   who dressed themselves up as Indians
   and dumped into Boston Harbor a load of tea.

First signer of the Declaration of Independence,
   he wrote his name so large and plain
   that ever since a John Hancock
   has meant the signing of a name.

Illness made him step down early,
   but he helped recoup finances by that time,
   from the devastation caused by Morris,
   though it was an uphill climb.

NATHANIEL GORHAM LOOKS FOR A KING OF AMERICA

President Nathaniel Gorham
(June-November 1786)

Nathaniel Gorham was a merchant,
   like five out of our ten.
   Four of them were lawyers,
   plus one planter businessman.

This native of Boston was chosen
   to fill out John Hancock's term
   when Hancock's health had failed him,
   and helped the Cincinnati scheme return.

He plotted for Prince Heinrich of Prussia
   to be brought in as their king,
   and when that royal plan failed,
   pushed for more presidential empowering.

SHAY'S
REBELLION

ARTHUR ST CLAIR

President Arthur St. Clair
(November 1786-November 1787)

Of a noble family from Scotland,
  St. Clair came to Pennsylvania from that distant shore
  after fighting in the conquest of Quebec City
  and under Washington in the Revolutionary War.
The largest landowner west of the Alleghenies,
  he later set up the North-West Territory,
  and then served as its Governor,
  in a financially successful story.

Wanting a stronger government to boost the worth of his land,
  he backed the plan for a new Constitution.
  and he found the excuse for such a change
  in the government's handling of Shay's Rebellion.
This revolt of debt-ridden farmers in western Massachusetts
  was in reaction to the bankruptcy of family farms.
  The farmers were defeated by state forces,
  but then went unpunished, which St. Clair viewed with alarm.

The result was Philadelphia's Federal Convention
  in the State House, called Independence Hall,
  which wrote up a new Constitution in secret,
  with stronger powers over all.
The President could propose legislation,
  use the army without a declaration of war,
  construe the Constitution,
  give pardons, send ambassadors, and more.

CYRUS GRIFFIN

Bill of Rights
Amendment the First
Amendment the Second
Amendment the Third
Amendment the Fourth
Amendment the Fifth
Amendment the Sixth
Amendment the Seventh
Amendment the Eighth
Amendment the Ninth
Amendment the Tenth

More to follow
through the years...

President Cyrus Griffin
(November 1787-November 1788)

The last of our first ten Presidents,
   Cyrus Griffin was of the landed gentry of Virginia,
   a judge trained at London's Middle Temple,
   wed to the Earl of Traquair's daughter Christina.

Under his leadership, the new Constitution was ratified
   and elections under the new system began.
   Patrick Henry claimed it would make the executive too strong
   so that a President one day might become a strong man.

And Thomas Jefferson said it indicated
   a degeneracy in the principles of liberty
   which he thought would take four centuries
   instead of four years to see.

Patrick Henry managed to add a Bill of Rights,
   when the Federalist Papers carried the day
   with arguments for ratification written by
   Alexander Hamilton, James Madison, and John Jay.

Conclusion

With George Washington in charge,
   people were taxed, though some gave a holler,
   to pay the states' debt to the wealthy for loans
   bought at only a few cents on the dollar.

The new Bank of the United States,
   representing private cash,
   was dominated by Robert Morris,
   bringing on the first Wall Street Crash.

Maclay exclaimed, "The President
   has become the dish clout of every dirty speculation
   as his name goes to wipe away blame
   and silence each objection."

Under John Adams, the Sedition Act outlawed
   Criticism of the Government,
   and several of its critics were fined
   or sent to jail in such an event.

But Richard Henry Lee had warned,
   "Lovers of liberty should never give
   rulers an atom of power not needed
   for society to safely live."

www.ingramcontent.com/pod-product-compliance
Lightning Source LLC
Chambersburg PA
CBHW060854270326

41934CB00002B/136